Afonso Daniel Sanana (born 01/02 December 1979) is an Angolan entrepreneur, a teacher with an MBA degree, a dedicated husband, father and brother residing in UAE, Dubai. He is interested in culture, politics and human development. This is his first work to be published.

I want to dedicate this book to all couples out there who no matter the difficulties, they still choose each other.

Afonso Daniel Sanana

QUALITIES OF A HAPPY MARRIAGE

AUSTIN MACAULEY PUBLISHERS™

LONDON • CAMBRIDGE • NEW YORK • SHARJAH

Table of Content

Preface	9
Part One: Introduction	11
Part Two: How Did We Get Here?	20
Part Three: Starting a Marriage	26
Part Four: Practical Applications	31
Part Five: Debunking the Toxicity of Marriages	40
Part Six: Real Conversation About Marriage	53
Part Seven: What Feeds Hatred in Relationships?	75
Part Eight: Important Qualities for a Happy Marriage	83
Loyalty	85
Responsibility	87
Respect	88
Faith	90
Confidence	91
Hope	93

Teamwork 94

Ending Note 95

Preface

We have lived amidst different centuries, and we have seen the many different courses of changes in our lives, too. Over the years, we have also seen couples around us, some married, some committed to each other, and some even divorced. With each new generation, there was a change in the quality of love and marital relationships, and as we move forward, we continue to find more and more information on what needs to be done to keep a marriage healthy.

It is important, specifically in the 21st century, to realise that the need for romantic love and satisfaction in a marital relationship is real. In the middle of these ever-changing times, there exists a responsibility for both the parties in a relationship; to learn how to guard and enhance their understanding of each other, more so, their love for each other. If you look around to learn from someone else's experience, who self-report their marriage as good, you can only question; what makes their marriage successful and worthwhile? In understanding what makes up a good marriage, there can be confusions; so in an attempt to narrate this the easy way, mention of a few qualities that most couples possess and exercise is very important.

It is even more real to understand that our love and marital relationships far outweigh other things of our lives. To live in a satisfying marital relationship is much more important for one's personal well-being than professional success, financial status, or even religion for some people.

When you voluntarily enter into a marriage contract with someone, you expect more life out of that relationship. You demand emotional satisfaction, endless support, lifelong love, and a stable future for your family. However, even being in such a relationship cannot guarantee any success, unless we focus on our personal qualities. So, in looking at the qualities of a good marriage, there is a need to focus more on cognitive and personal characteristics of both the parties. However, since each person varies with their beliefs, attitude, and general way of life, a few common qualities can be talked about; ones that really help bring success in a marital relationship.

In this book, the focus remains on the importance of a good marriage, what are the negative, toxic aspects in a marriage, how you can guard your relationship practicing a few qualities, how you can bridge the gap between your struggling relationships, and self-report that your marital relationship is good.

If your relationship is new or if it has already passed the test of time, know that you may not be doing some things right. However, with the right manual, you can get past the gloomy days in your marriage and reconnect with your partner. That is to say, you are the creator of your happiness, and at any point in life, you and your partner can get better as a team.

Part One: Introduction

We're born alone, we live alone, we die alone. Only through our love and friendship can we create the illusion for a moment that we're not alone. — Orson Welles

We see and experience the originality of this world through our own eyes, we also hold our experiences within ourselves. When we are born alone, and when we die alone, why is there a need for someone else amidst this phase? Why do we need to live with others to create momentary illusions for ourselves, to not feel alone, or to not exhaust ourselves with the familiarity or uncertainty of this world? Do we need people around us so we can share our thoughts and experiences with them, so we can understand things from varying perspectives, so we can truly live with support?

People, even if they share the same experiences as us, can only make us wonder what it is like to live like them. We can only understand others vicariously, using our own thoughts. But as we continue to spend time around them, we slowly understand why we need those people around us.

So, even if we are made to die alone, we need someone by our side. The time we spend in between the time of our life and death needs us to have someone; family, love, friendship.

This someone is meant to be there for us emotionally, spiritually and physically; someone we can tend to in times of need, someone whom we can share our happiness with, and divide our problems.

In your life, you must have also seen your parents, wondered how they had lived a long time being with each other. If they had ever faced the test of time, you must have also wondered why there is a need for someone else. It is inevitable you hadn't seen anyone else's experience and formed a meaning out of it to avoid being in that situation.

But, with each individual, the story varies. Experiences, values, qualities, and perceptions are different for everyone. How would you live if you were to live alone? You wouldn't progress. You wouldn't change. It is exactly why we need pairing; when we partner with someone different than us, life's originality becomes apparent. It builds for us an experience that is very real, something that can offer to us more wisdom.

So, to realise that life is ephemeral for anyone alive, and for as long as you live, you need someone you can partner. Now, your family, while they are the closest to you, can only do so much for you. Your friends or your partner can add into your personal development, emotional stability, and occupational success. But, the most important role is that of a partner. Someone you love or admire can set the foundational basis of your life, success, and individuality.

I often get asked what I think love is, or why I need to love someone. There are different ways I can transform feelings of love into words, and it is a feeling defined differently by each individual. Each time, it is right in its own way. To me, *love is to never give up*, and this book is all that is about.

Love is the very feeling that builds the foundation of a marital relationship. And while the legal meaning of a marriage contract is to live together, it is much more real and deeper than most different relationships. It requires certain attributes and qualities, most of all, it needs love to prosper successfully.

A happy marriage is a goal of every couple; finding an ideal partner as our soul mate and our better half is a hope, a dream, and a search that quite a lot of people find difficulty in.

Building a strong and lasting marriage is not easy, but it isn't impossible either. We still see many couples living in their happy marriages; others who continue to celebrate their Silver, Pearl, Ruby, Golden, and Diamond Wedding Anniversaries, don't they?

The question is, is it possible for two people to live together happily for a long time? Unfortunately for many, living together happily is only possible in fairy tales, or in romantic movies. There are couples whom some of us even envy, as their marriage looks really happy as we often see in fairy tales.

Honestly, this only happens because they make continuous and selfless efforts to gain maintain the relationship with the person they have married. However, these efforts aren't supposed to be an on and off situation, "It takes commitment, time, and dedication."

Regardless of the divorce ratio currently, we should agree that no one marries someone thinking we aren't going to be together one day. Marriage isn't just a contract, it is a vow, a promise that isn't supposed to go empty. It is filled with emotions, expectations and efforts. It is tied with the knot of love and care, and is supposed to stay that way till the end. However, marriages do fall apart, people do end up not wanting to stay together. But why is that?

Think of the last happily married couple you know, what did they do to make their marriage work? What did they have that kept them married and committed to each other? Marriage has long been thought to be the ultimate show of love and devotion between two people. In fact, the dictionary states that marriage is a voluntary union of a man and a woman, under conditions sanctioned by law so that a legitimate family unit is formed and established. Whether or not one agrees with this definition: marriage still comes down to making a relationship public, official, legal and permanent. In theory, this union will last until death or law brings you apart.

We would argue that marriage is a mind-set—a perspective that only needs great care, understanding and focus. Well, the reality is much diverse! Marriage is supposed to join two people, two gene pools, and two families to establish two futures together for the generations to come.

Marriage isn't something you give up on, it is ought to be fought for and seen with an eternal perspective on how this all fits together and how the institution was designed. Marriage always has been seen as the only source of family foundation. We need to re-adjust our attitudes about marriage and save the institution that fails as often as it succeeds.

In the world of today, the problems of society mainly take place because of the degradation of families. We are forgetting the fundamental principal of any well-structured society: A happy family is the foundation of a stable society.

A key concept in social sciences and especially in demography and sociology is that the family is generally considered as an important social institution and a place for much of a person's social activity.

The family is generally regarded as a major social institution and a locus of much of a person's social activity.

It is generally assumed today that modern family undergo significant transformations in its structure.

So, how is it then that more marriages than ever before are ending in divorce and shattering families across the globe? The statistics are alarming! According to the Centre for Disease Control and Prevention, in the United States there is one divorce approximately every 36 seconds*. That's nearly 2,400 divorces per day, 16,800 divorces per week and 876,000 divorces a year. Just in UAE where I live, reports state that the net divorce rate between UAE population in the Emirate, whether both spouses are UAE nationals or not, reached last year to 12.5 for each one thousand UAE couples. In Angola, where I come from, 45% of the hundred couples that get married, end up in divorce.

It's no secret that debates and struggles over marriage and family issues have increased over the recent years. What has happened in recent generations that caused this shift and made marriage less about "forever" and more about "for right now as long as I can take it"? My question is, since when did marriage vows cease to matter? Seems to me that more often than not, marriage is taken lightly and then given up on as soon as challenges surface; mostly because the relationship becomes less exciting when responsibilities emerge. The reality is simple—marriage is hard and we need to accept that. It isn't just fairy tales and rainbows. It's always been hard and that hasn't changed and isn't going to change ever either. Think about it, you enter into a union that can last up to seven or eight decades. That's a long time, and during that time a lot is bound to happen. Romantic love increases or decreases, life events change people, personalities change as people age, mature, grow, and develop; moreover, their likes and dislikes change, bodies change. And often time over time, people find themselves growing apart.

Covey Stephen R. states that movies and reality TV shows have generally shaped us to believe that we are not responsible, that we are merely a product of our feelings. But the script does not describe the entire reality.

So often we assume that the fairy tale exists. Somehow, we've managed to convince ourselves that our most intimate relationships should always feel easy and be free from conflict or difference of opinion. We look for "the one and only" and jump into marriage and then wonder why it feels hard.

I always believe that love's job ends on the day you sign the paper or the day we say I do, afterwards is a relation that needs more than just love to survive. It requires compromise, commitment, hope, dedication, understanding, loyalty, trust, responsibility and team work.

We have unrealistic expectations of what our relationship is supposed to look like 100% of the time and then when it falls short of our lofty assumptions, it feels hard and we look to jump out of the ship before it sinks and drowns us as well. We tend to believe that we aren't wrong for expecting and not putting in enough efforts. For us, it is always the other person who's wrong. We'd never even agree that we can have toxic traits as well. This is because we often forget that marriage is a mutually dependent relationship where we need to combine our own efforts with our partners to achieve the greatness of it.

We look at our friends and neighbours' relationships and assume that the grass really is greener on the other side. That is just not so.

The grass is not greener on the other side until you decide to water it daily.

We need to let go of the fantasy of perfection and stick close to the fantasy of perfection within our efforts. We need to take some of the traditional values of old-school marriage and combine what was working while giving attention to the challenges of today and build something new and unique that will actually function for us. We need to decide today whether we're willing to bring conscious awareness back in our marriages and be willing to do whatever it takes to protect and nurture our relationship forever. A healthy marriage takes two people who are committed to pursue and intentionally engage in the process of creating a healthy marriage and that will take time, patience and dedication. As they say, it's a marathon and not a sprint. People grow and change, circumstances alter and consequently, a marriage lasts only when those involved have a certain amount of flexibility and ability to adjust and evolve when a new situation arises. A marriage will never stay the same as it was when it started. It is bound to change. Therefore, the sense of welcoming and understanding change is what needs to be more common. If change wasn't bound to happen, it would suffocate both the partners and you'd be so bored and stagnant, there is very little chance it would survive. We need to accept that change is not a threat—it's an opportunity to learn, grow and progress. Your relationship should be dynamic and adaptable—not unchanged and unchallenged. We need to look into our relation as prestigiously throughout our lives as we did when it started. There is a Portuguese quote that says "whoever runs for fun never gets tired".

We should know that no marriage is perfect or free from conflict. So what makes some couples exceptionally successful in their marriage while others struggle to make it just work? Is there a secret formula for a successful marriage? What successful life coping skills are used for those couples that seem to be able to calm down any of the storms that life throws their way? How can you cope with difficulties that invariably rise and how can you keep the spark alive?

These are some of the questions we aim to answer in this book. Now more than ever there seems to be an attack on marriages and families. We know that a successful relationship calls for consistent and diligent efforts from both the sides. Building a strong marriage is a skill that can be learned but it requires commitment, devotion and a willingness to set aside your own interests for the sake of your significant other and the relationship.

There are many qualities that go into a successful marriage that we want to cover, and although this is not a comprehensive list some are as follows: love, faith, hope, forgiveness, loyalty, respect, confidence, responsibility, common mission, team work, compassion and humour. Our knowledge is imperfect, our wisdom limited, and various topics will have a vast difference of opinions depending on who you ask. So, you as the reader will be charged with the shared responsibility of taking the information on the following pages and deciding the best route for adapting it into your life, your marriage and your perspective of life.

Part Two:
How Did We Get Here?

Singles perceive that their lives are more freedom-driven, independent, and socially active. They also think that the profusion of casual relationship options just makes their search for an official partner very narrow and superficial. With an intention to stay in a relationship, singles presume that conducting a relationship means giving up, for the most part, on their freedom. It is this perception that builds up complexities in the former stages, urging many to not give up on their independent lives at all. Singles also come across relationship stories that do not best fit their personal principles, often, many learn about relationship toxicity and tend to stay afar from engaging in any serious relationships. Besides, it is also common for singles to assume that a serious relationship will not feed their independence, self-growth, careers, and therefore, not divulge into romantic relationships to avoid these failures.

Romantic relationships require a combination of diversity and flexibility, however with restrictions. Partners in relationships cannot have everything they want because it is not healthy, romantically. Adopting a moderate pattern serves partners well, you may also need to go on little breaks to romantically flourish. Singles, too, have to realise that while there may be intricacy of their conflicting desires and ways of life, there will be a combination of balance and flexibility in a serious relationship, when maintained well.

A romantic relationship or a contractual marriage are not a way towards a bumpy road that'll be over once you change the route. The thing is, there are no changing of routes ever, if you're looking for a happy lasting marriage that is! There are no quick and easy paths to a successful and committed marriage. Those who have survived to an extent that they're able to tell the tale will tell you that it's a long road with ups and downs, bumps and bruises, along with several tears and laughter. It takes patience, work, love, and constant action. Happy marriages don't just happen on their own. They are fought for and the effort that they require is ongoing. It's a consistent decision made by both partners to "show up" for their marriage and partner.

Since the beginning of time, marriage has brought together people and formed family units. We were meant to be together in pairs. Humans were never supposed to live alone without any partner. We aren't made that way either. However, the recent times have changed and statistics show that nowadays people are more cynical about marriage than ever before. The youth of today is debunking trends that have been in place for decades. While for some, change may be good and trends may come and go, it's still concerning when we see it affecting something as traditional and steadfast as marriage. Marriage is not just a tradition; it is a need and a part of our nature. But it seems like it's becoming increasingly more difficult from the get-go for young people to fall in love, get married, and have enduring relationships that will last the test of time.

What's changed in recent decades? It used to be that marriage was a good sign of an individual finally reaching adulthood; it was one of the main indicators. However, that has changed in recent years and studies suggest that the youth no longer look at marriage as an indicator of adulthood and the median age of people getting married for the first time is on the rise.

Lifestyle choices in the early life seem to also coincide with the success of the marriage and the views that the individual has on marriage and the importance of marriage. (Carroll, Willoughby, Badger, Nelson, Barry & Madsen, 2007.)

It used to be that individuals went from adolescence to adulthood through marriage. Not anymore, though. We now have given individuals a period of life between childhood and adulthood that we've coined "emerging adulthood" (Arnett 2000) which now extends upwards of 10 years from when an individual sees themselves as an adult but hasn't taken on adult responsibility, like marriage and a family. So what does this delayed period of someone being single have to do with his or her perceptions and commitment to marriage? How does it change their preparation for marriage?

Because of the erosion of courting and dating culture that young people are currently a part of, in comparison to those cultures in previous generations, we see a rise in pessimism towards marriage. In previous generations people used to put their relationships before themselves. They sacrificed for the relationship and kept the joint partnership and wellbeing of both people at the forefront of their minds when making decisions. Unfortunately, this is not what we see today. Instead, the tendency of focusing on individual successes has become more of a priority; be it financial independence or achieving personal milestones, a couple making their way through this world and those milestones together has, indeed, become rare.

The pessimism we see these days isn't about marriage in itself. Most of the youth still believes in the importance·and power of marriage and a family life.

Sadly, the current generation has experienced pain and trauma more frequently than the generations that have passed by. Growing up with broken hearts and broken families has left them second-guessing the concept of love and marriage. Now, because these emerging adults are growing up in a world that is littered with failed marriages and broken relationships, they view the possibility of finding a long-lasting, romantic comedy sort of relationship and marriage impossible or as the exception to the norm instead of the norm. Because of this, these young adults are coming from a place and mind-set which prepares them for divorce before preparing them for marriage. They are going into these relationships with the expectation of failure and the eventual exit of the relationship instead of the older generations view of "we are in this together", "we are going to put in the work necessary to make this marriage work", "we are committed to each other, no matter what", "in sickness and in health—till death do us apart".

This new pattern of thinking during the period of singleness is now accepted and is actually starting to be seen as a necessary period of one's life, or a certain stepping stone to marriage. Many these days are actually putting off marriage phase on purpose so that they can "fully experience the single life" before they settle down and get married.

Another thinking pattern has emerged that has changed the culture of marriage is financial success or being financially independent. Before this generation, people believed that marriage could be alongside other aspects of life. For example, finishing education, working hard at our jobs or settling into a long-term career, buying a house and working to provide for your family. However, these days, there is a trend where young people are putting off marriage until they view themselves as successful or financially independent. Finally, after achieving certain educational or career milestones they might then and only then think that they can now "afford" a marriage. But as any parent can attest, if you ever wait until you can afford to have children—you will never have children. The same can be said for marriage.

Previously, the trend was to get married, care for your spouse, provide for your family and nurture your children. All of these things were a duty to serve and nurture someone else. Ever since this trend has changed, the youth has placed their attention back to themselves; their personal interests, self-reliance and independence are in the forefront. This is why the youth is delaying marriage, to pursue independence. This will only further complicate a marriage as two entirely independent people will finally come together when they've forgotten how to work as a team and work towards achieving goals together instead progressing alone.

Again, we see the tendency to put oneself and personal goals and milestones ahead of the partnership of marriage. Long gone are the milestones of marriage—now they have become milestones that must be reached before marriage can even be considered. Perhaps in the newly "divorce prepared" generation, its simple mathematics:

The youth doesn't want to enter into marriage until they are financially ready to potentially be able to get divorced.

25

Part Three:
Starting a Marriage

Okay, so you've managed to mature out of your "single life" and "emerging adulthood" nonsense, and now you finally believe that you're ready to live your life with someone. You've also found "the one" and you've decided to get married. Great! Congratulations! Well done! You've crossed the hard path of trying to become the best version of yourself with wisdom, maturity and life experience. You've also crossed the hard path of finding someone whom you love and want to spend the rest of your life with (in theory). You're smitten and ready to settle down and create a life with someone else. Fantastic!

But you're a little worried now, aren't you? It's a big step and you have this constant thought in your head asking you what if you mess up? What then? You worry if someday you might just stand and ask yourself what now? How do you manage to build and work towards the best marriage of all time? How do you manage to keep yourself from being another statistic of a failed marriage?

Worry not, let's dive into what might make a fabulous marriage.

The good news is, it appears that you have the ability to love. This is because you're already worried and trying to make it work even before it has started. We don't say that lightly either. Social science experiments and surveys have found that a person's ability to love and communicate, directly correlate with the happiness of their marriage. One's ability to love can be simplified down to how one expresses, asserts or defines his or her importance and the importance of others in an intimate as well as a non-intimate relationship. (L'Abate, 1997, pg. 4). Love is also defined by some as the ability to be emotionally available to self and others especially in times of need. Meaning—when loved ones are hurt or are fearful of being hurt—we are there with no expectation of performance, problem solving, production, or perfection. Basically, the ability to love requires a certain amount of self-worth or personal security and a cherished regard for others.

Personal security or self-worth is important in an intimate relationship because the relationship is not all about you. You have to have a certain amount of vulnerability and openness to possibly being hurt in order to make a lasting commitment to someone else. You have to have enough self-worth to fight the common urge to avoid potential rejection. Fear of rejection often dictates the behaviour and decisions of those who are not secure enough in who they are and allow themselves to be swayed by the threat of a heartbreak.

When someone goes into a relationship with a sense of care about others instead of themself; it opens the doors to fostering love, commitment, kindness, compassion, openness, forgiveness, fairness, and sacrifice among other personal virtues. It's not always easy and requires a certain amount of maturity to let the needs of someone else become equal or even more important than your own.

Another important aspect in having a healthy marriage is the ability to communicate. Many marriages that could have and probably should had been saved and repaired ended because of one or both participants' inability to properly communicate with each other.

Communication is basically the ability to interact with others in a way that allows you to solve problems, bargain, and reach a consensus while still respecting the rights of all parties. The ability to communicate rests squarely on the shoulders of one's ability to love. Communication like so many other important aspects of a marriage is a skill that can be learned. It takes patience and practice, but one can become an expert communicator if the desire is there. The first of two core aspects of communication involves empathetic listening where one makes the other feel valued and understood. We cannot emphasise enough over the value of good listening skills. Listening doesn't just mean you're all ears to someone venting their heart out to you, it also means you're understanding their situation and are there for them no matter what.

The second part of effective communication is clearly sending messages to each other. Communication generally starts to break down not when two people can't form words, sentences and ideas to each other, but usually it happens when the background issues keep people from being open, honest, genuine and sincere in their verbal communication with each other. If we can't say what we mean and mean what we say while still respecting the perspectives, feelings and emotions of others—the relationship breaks down. Trust and intimacy

Part Four:
Practical Applications

We all know that happiness is fleeting. It isn't constant. There are always going to be moments where you'll be happy and moments where you'll be sad. The most successful couples know that and prepare for it. They look for ways to bring happiness back into their marriage and partnership in rough times. It is said, if there's a will, there's a way. These couples are always willing to try new things. They know that if they put in the same effort they did before, they'd get the same positive results. If one problem solving approach doesn't work, they get to work on another. It's an ever-changing evolution of partnership. The main point is to be willing enough to change your own attitude and thinking. What now is believed to be compromise or sacrifice, were once said to be efforts to stay together. What is wrong in moulding yourself a bit in the name of love, anyway? People's negative thoughts create negative attitudes and negative behaviours. The same can be said for the positive side. Sometimes all it takes is a change in thought or attitude to completely change a situation. A recent article of Psychology Today suggested there should be a five-to-one ratio of positive to negative thoughts, feelings and behaviours towards your spouse and marriage.

Another school of thought stands by their assessment that marriages should be treated like a bank account. They also back up the five-to-one ratio given above. They further clarify by saying: "Nearly 70% of marital conflicts are perpetual and unresolvable—they're ongoing and last the couple's entire lifetime… **A couple that has at least five times more positive interactions than negative ones will ultimately succeed.** Happy marriages, thus, aren't conflict-free, they're just infused with *more* positivity than negativity. This reserve of positivity acts as a buffer that mitigates and defuses the love-deteriorating effects of a couple's conflicts—absorbing these negative ripples and keeping them from spreading and overwhelming the relationship."

They use the above ratio with the instituted "relationship bank account" which is a fascinating idea. Every time you do something negative in your relationship, it's withdrawal. Like money draining to zero in your account, the closer you get to zero, the more anxiety, frustration and burden you bear with each following withdrawal. On the flip side, every positive interaction, word, physical touch etc. is a deposit. When you have ample funds, you don't worry and fret about the withdrawals coming out. For them, a fight is nothing more than a fight and does not carry the potential to break a relationship. It's not that the happy couple is withdrawing any less than the unhappy couple; it's just that they have more to withdraw from.

When you aren't stressed, burdened and anxious over every little aspect of your relationship, things have a tendency of just going smoother and easier. You can be more relaxed about potential conflicts because you know it won't escalate. You know there's no point in keeping your guards up. So you can be real. It's okay for you to show and express real emotion, and even rationally tell yourself to back down when you know one of these little arguments are starting to get more heated than necessary. You are more willing to stop fighting and compromise because you want to get back to the good part…and you believe all this negative energy is just a waste of your time.

It has also become very apparent that the amount of fun a couple has together as well as the depth of their friendship will be a great indicator of how the couple will be fair to each other in long-term. Happy marriages are based on a deep friendship which is filled with purity and simplicity. In fact, most people who have been experiencing issues in their marriage focus more on fixing their friendship than just the issue at hand. This act then helps reduce the risk of developing further problems.

Being friends in a marriage is the most beautiful thing. There's an old belief that says, "Love is friendship on fire." A lot of couples who have a hard time working directly on their marriage such as sitting down and talking about their issues for 30 minutes a day or going to couples counselling (we don't necessarily think that's a bad idea), are unaware of how these little positive interactions and deposits can make a relationship stronger.

Movies and romantic fantasies have forced people to believe that over-dramatic attempts that involve a materialistic approach are the reason love stays in the air. However, a materialistic approach such as buying flowers or gifts for your significant other isn't what keeps them close, it's the thought and effort behind it.

Love isn't something you can buy, rent, or barter with.

The surety of love can only be given through your actions, considerations and in the reflection of your eyes.

Another point that should be made is the fallacy in expecting your spouse to be a certain person, do certain things, act in a certain way or comply with your lofty expectations if you yourself are not willing to do, be, act, or comply. If you want a certain mate, you've got to be willing to be that certain mate. You cannot simply ask for a certain quality you yourself do not possess. Sounds simple, but so many couples out there forget this basic fundamental point and then wonder why things aren't jiving the way they anticipated.

We can't talk about qualities of a happy marriage without talking about sex and physical intimacy. Expectations regarding sex have been known to cause huge problems in a marriage. Not every partner wants to have sex all the time and that's okay. Going into a marriage and realising that sex is going to ebb and flow and change while a relationship will go a long way in helping prevent sex being one of the main causes of relationship issues. You aren't necessarily attracted to your partner with the same intensity throughout the relationship. There's going to be fluctuation and it's completely normal. With time passing and life making its way, you'd come to realise that your priorities are bound to change as well. Sometimes, career is going to be your main focus, sometimes it's going to be family and sometimes it's going to be the excitement in your marriage. Nonetheless, each of them is still going to be in your priority list. It's just that, what's on the top is going to change. Your sexual desire changes according to your emotional state, physical health, and your feelings of connection to your partner. There are going to be periods where the two of you will be having great sex and even regular sex. There will also be periods where your sex life is less central to your relationship and takes a back seat to the other things going on in your life. There may even be times when one or both of you are dissatisfied with the state of your sexual connection. This is normal as well. It shouldn't be ignored, but dissatisfaction with your sex life isn't a permanent thing or a cause for divorce. It's normal and can be worked through.

That being said, you should be having regular sex with your partner. It increases intimacy, connection and is an important part of the relationship, just not the only part of the relationship that matters. Relationships have to move forward and progress or they will eventually die. The longer we are with our partners, the more comfortable we become and it can make even the hottest spark start to wane and die after some time. Many couples find in the first part of their relationship that they can't get enough of each other. The sex is great and when one partner comes home after a long day, the other partner is excited to see them and may greet them with a passionate kiss. After a time, that passionate kiss may turn into a small peck on the check and then may further digress into the other partner not even looking up from what they are doing when their partner comes walking through the door. The more casual and mundane the marriage becomes, the more risk there is in developing problems. It's impractical to assume that marriage will always have the same twitter-pated excitement and lust like it did in the beginning, but we've still got to do a better job of protecting the intimacy.

Intimacy isn't just about sex and passion isn't just about doing it in every room of the house. The habits you form in the bedroom will change and age just like you. What is healthy and normal for your relationship in regards to passion and intimacy may not be what's normal and healthy for someone else. What gets us going and what works for us is going to be as different as our relationships are. For some, it may be coming home to a clean house maybe that will be what gets them going. For others, it may be a dramatic sign of romance like a candle-lit bath with soft music and chocolate. Whereas for some, the greatest display of passion might be their spouse jumping to their defence during the next conflict with a neighbour. It's different for everyone, but every couple generally knows what works for them. Be confident in your knowledge that things may change over time but it doesn't make it any less fun or exciting. Intimacy with your partner comes in many shapes, sizes and forms and may not include sex at all, for some it may be as simple as deep conversation or cuddling on the couch.

A study on men and their infidelity states that nearly half of all men who cheated reported it was because of emotional dissatisfaction and not because of sex. (That means that every time your partner feels unappreciated, unneeded, or disconnected—they become vulnerable to the advances of the opposite sex that's willing to send them lustful glances and probably shower them with kind words and sweet nothings.)

How can we better protect our marriages from straying or infidelity? There are multiple tactics that probably should be used in conjunction with each other. Some we have already covered and others we will try to cover as well.

We should not forget to thank our partners for the little things and should also compliment them whenever possible. In this world of stress and pressure, we cannot deny that we all are suckers for kindness, gestures and gratitude. It's easy to feel unappreciated and undervalued when our partner forgets to notice the good we are trying to do. This plays a huge role in the success of the "relationship bank account" method we discussed earlier. Every time you make a positive deposit, it's going to strengthen your relationship. It's pretty easy to stop noticing what your partner does and only notice what you do. Often times we start trying to keep score. "I took out the garbage". "I put the kids to bed." "I initiated sex the last 17 times." So on and so forth. This habit is easy to start and harder to break. It will only work to erode your relationship over time and help build frustration, expectation, negativity and resentment.

If you feel like you have to keep score, why not keep a positive score? It is better to notice and appreciate the positive things your partner does. It doesn't only build a positive environment, but works as reverse psychology as well. For example, if your partner did something you want them to do more often, appreciate them for it, reward them for it as well. It will work wonders. Notice those things, and just like that, your relationship will start to improve. You are making those positive deposits every day and soon you will have a flushed account that will able to withstand a few withdrawals with very little worry.

One of the simplest tools of a successful relationship is a basic attribute that we, unfortunately, now find rarely:

kindness. We tend to treat our loved ones in the worst possible way. This is because we can't always take our aggression and frustration out on those who caused it (bad boss, bad neighbour, bad financial advisor) – instead, they become the collateral damage. But we need to understand that the ones who loves us, aren't supposed to be our punching bag. They see us at our worst and still love us and we usually get away with the way we treat them.

Honestly, we could save ourselves so much pain and heartache if we'd just change our approach and look for ways to make our partner happy on a daily basis. Why aren't we treating the ones we hold most dear, better than we are willing to treat the mailman or cashier at the store? Why should those strangers get better from us than those who were willing to hitch their wagon for us and believed in us and our forever? Sometimes, that means we have to sacrifice for our partner, our best friend. We watch the lame romantic comedy she's been dying to see, or we sit through another torturous round of history trivia because that's what he's into. Basically, we do things for our partner and find joy in seeing them happy.

Here comes the toughest part: Maintaining honesty with your partner even when it's not going to "work out well for you" is important. Trust can take years to build but moments to destroy and once destroyed, there's really no easy way back to it. Let's admit, all of us make mistakes. Sometimes, it's over-spending, sometimes some sort of cheating, or maybe you just scratched your partner's brand-new car. Regardless the issue, you will always fare better with your partner if you decide to deal with the situation with honesty.

Honesty also matters when it comes to the state of your relationship. If you feel like things aren't where they should be or you aren't on-track, speak up about it. Be honest. Let your partner know how you are feeling instead of just pretending like everything is fine or ignoring the issue. Letting it slide isn't really an option, it will just pile up and explode one day, causing situations to escalate.

Another tip that's come in handy for many couples is to let it go. Seriously, let it go. Not every single little thing that comes up needs to be dealt with and handled. Sometimes the best way to address a problem is to just walk away from it. Not every mistake was meant to happen, not every insult was intended. Pick and choose your battles and let the rest go as much as possible. Forget more. Forgive more. Remind yourself why you married this person, what you love about them and practice biting your tongue more and let go of your need to get the last word in. There shouldn't really be any kind of competition between the two of you. Your partner is feeling the same stresses, pressures and distractions that you are in. Cut them and yourself some slack. Let a certain amount of things pass away without mentioning them. You have to really let it pass through and let it go instead of just choosing not to say something and then letting it fester and build up more resentment for you. Picking and choosing your battles is an art. It will take time to practice this new skill but it's a skill worth having.

Part Five:
Debunking the Toxicity
of Marriages

Following the common beliefs held by the young's of today, this section will divulge into the reality of married life. It will debunk the very idea that failed marriages of past or broken marriages in the family do not set the base same for everyone. There, however, are different behavioural patterns and characteristics that help make a marriage successful.

As soon as your engagement ring slipped, you are inundated with hundreds of questions about how your relationship is going on or how it should be. The family and friends tell you what you should and shouldn't do. Your relationships ultimately determine your views on interpersonal relationships, and some of these general beliefs can be toxic for you, thinking process and relation as well. They misled the couple or, worse, convinced them that their marriage was hopeless.

These myths have destroyed countless healthy relationships simply because the couple thought it was fundamentally wrong. Toxic feelings can manifest as suspicion, criticism, dissatisfaction, attacks, pessimism, dissatisfaction, perfectionism, and excessive tension. All of these actions can knock you out (including your partner).

It is essential to maintain a positive attitude in marriage. No one can avoid all toxic thoughts. Less toxic thoughts about your spouse will make your marriage happier. Spend time with your partner and reconnect. Be positive and refuse to let go of toxic opportunities. You can also talk to your close friend or qualified counsellor about your concerns to let these toxic thoughts. If you are hesitant to speak to others about it, then look for the positive side. For some couples, this simple step can be revolutionary. This includes trying new ways of thinking that can find good things for your partner and offer positive solutions to your problems. Look beyond the negative qualities of your spouse and look for kindness. Also, you can reject to be a victim. No matter what situation you face, no matter how difficult it is, you will not fall victim. Self-pity is likely to diminish you and your relationship. Don't let it ruin your attitude and your marriage.

Nothing can stop a good attitude from emerging better than good grudges. Annoyances and bitterness are toxins of positive thinking. Therefore, you must give up feeling bad in the hope of a better attitude, no matter how fair it may seem. Give to yourself and your marriage a little grace. Toxic attitudes and feelings can form habits, so it is difficult to get rid of this pattern. Give yourself a race on the way. Remember that each new day offers a new opportunity to start over. Every day, your efforts to improve your attitude bring you closer to the marriage you want.

Without clear labels, there are many types of unwanted relationships, but the actual definition of a toxic relationship is an unsafe, ineffective relationship between two or more.

This is different from negligence, dysfunction, relationship, or other relationships that do not work at all because it is not safe to stay physically or emotionally.

Toxic relationships remove negative feelings, but toxic and passive relationships are characterised by negative behaviour that is consistent or normal in the relationship. This behaviour includes (but is not limited to) jealousy, insults, humiliation, and shouting. These involve domination, control, narcissism, and insecurity, which can cause emotional or even physical harm. In this relationship, expectations about the role that everyone often plays are uneven; for example, one is given, and the other takes.

Toxic relationships affect you on countless points. They affect your psychology and make you constantly ask what you do and who you are. They can make you ask because your intuition tells you one thing and your brains tell you another (hint: always hold on to intuition). When you are told that you are insane, wrong, or unable to live alone, thus, it also affects your self-confidence. And because you feel compelled to do so, you also see a clear manifestation of toxic effects. You may feel feverish or depressed. You may not want to get up one day because this relationship affects your thinking, work, and personal lives. You may even begin to hate yourselves because you are not true to yourselves, especially when you feel you are violating your beliefs and values.

Early Warning: Detect a Toxic Relationship

To find out what a toxic relationship looks like, look at the following examples:

- A partner who devalues your contribution and claims that you are "worthless".
- A partner who is very jealous of your friends and damages your reputation.
- A partner separates you from other friends or family by lying.
- A partner who harshly criticise you. They might say, "You are too dumb; you can never do anything."
- A partner who does not allow you to behave or act with your family members.
- A relationship where all your energy is invested in the relationship, and still, you feel tired.
- A relationship that saddles you the most or all the time.

Marriage Is Always Equal

Some therapists and counsellors will tell you that a good marriage requires the same kind of reciprocal nature. "You're scratching my back; I'm scratching yours." "You help clean the house, and I help clean the trash." This forces the couple in response to some unwritten agreement in return for some word or behaviour.

Keep track of who did what, with whom has the real problem in married life. Unplug the dishwasher during payment, as the couple does not like the second cooked. A happy marriage consists of positive emotions, not an ideal 50/50 split.

In a toxic relationship, this unspoken or vague contract fills with resentment and anger. When a couple writes a "contract" about who does what, it is no longer unconditional love and mutual support. It becomes a "keeping score".

Sometimes you have to do more than just be fair in your marriage. Maybe your wife is going back to school, or your husband is having business meetings that could give her a great promotion. They usually do the same when you face a challenge. It is not about equality in everything; it is about loving them and work together to keep things going. Sometimes it does not seem fair. This does not mean that you have to do everything for your partner, waiting for your partner to do everything for you. It is also toxic. If you think things are unfair for a while, don't stick to it. Go to your partner and tell them you think you are doing a lot. If it helps you solve any problems, it will make you feel better—no scorecard required to make you feel good.

Similarly, healthy relationships, such as a healthy office building or house, also depend on a positive flow of energy. In my limited sense, positive thinking offers a way to maintain a flow of positive energy and minimise negative energy. Positive energy, which expresses enthusiasm, interest in others, thanks, gratitude, and care, brings happiness. Negative energy weakens happiness. Thus, these principles apply to all relationships. Remove negative energy and add positive energy to everyone who interacts with you: your loved ones—lovers, spouses, children, the elderly, and your friends and colleagues.

Spreading negative energy in a relationship invites tension and depression, and triggers annoyance at your attitude increases toxicity that will make to keep distant from your partner. On the other hand, by stimulating a positive flow of energy during communication, makes you attractive towards your partner.

"Clear the Clutter. Remove Anything You Don't Like."

In the house, it is easy to notice the clutter, for example, on the trash can on your working desk. But what interferes with your relationships? A small number of words can cause a lot of mess and create big trouble.

"Have a Good Air and Good Light."

Good relations must need a breathing space. With your partner, a clear division of your roles will create space and boundaries. Together with the partner, it provides a space where you can make your own decisions. With lovers and spouses, it is essential that everyone has their time and that everyone has their views and activities.

Good relationships also develop with interest and light of positivity. It is essential to achieve harmony, appreciate, share laughter, notice, praise, and share feelings.

"Tone: Always Be Mindful of the Feel of Your Home."

Emphasise the tone of voice or ignore the negative dissonance that is obvious to the partner. All the tones of "I'm fine, you're wrong," tell you that Eric Berne once said, "I'm all right; you're not right." The same goes for annoyance, frustration, sarcasm, anger, or anger.

Anxiety is another form of emotional disturbance. Although anxiety can occasionally warn of problems that need attention, frequent energy, or persistent anxiety may indicate a mental pattern that you may want to change.

Criticism is a reliable way to pass on negative energy to your partner. Criticism, especially when it is presented in a boring or irritated tone, conveys the message "you are not well" message. The request is acceptable if there are genuine needs or questions. Demands are not, including subtle comments like "I need you to..." or "I would like you to..." Requests have a question in them: "How would you fell about...?" Or "Could you...please?"

Don't Allow Yourself to Be Brought Down by Their Negative Energy.

"Rachel, my husband, has been complaining for a long time and is always in a bad mood. He found out that everything was bad and was constantly frustrated. I don't know how to help him or sometimes live with him, which I don't want." It's spoiling my and my children's lives. What should I do to be positive, given his strong negative energy?"

It is tough to live with a negative person. They can usually be depressed or negative. They are addicted or wrapped to their bad energy, so they can't see how miserable had made other's lives, so you should let alone relieve the toxicity on others. They even laugh at your positive attitude or call you naive when you see the good in people and things.

If you've ever tried to talk to them and have only met the downsides, you need to consult a doctor in the first place. To maintain a positive position and protect your negative spouse from negative influences, you must first understand that your positive energy is everything; I mean everything!

For you: When you feel positive and good, you not only attract more good things but when you feel alive, and it's become easier to cope with stressful events. Keeping a positive flow is the most important thing you can do for yourself and your relationship.

For your partner: Feeling also puts you in a better position to help your partner. In 2003, I began offering emotional distress and crisis relief on the site of volunteer services, and I continued for four years. I quickly realised that if I helped people successfully, I wouldn't be able to carry negative energy. I have discovered many tips on how to be active and clear and help thousands of people in need without being affected. After that, I really felt more positive and fulfilled.

The powerful secrets I have learned are useful to me and will hopefully help them avoid negative influences.

Ways to Stay Positive and Protect Yourself from the Negativity of Your Spouse

Avoid Using Negative Emotions.

You are usually equal in your feelings to communicate with and connect with your partner. For example, if your partner is bothering something, you can reflect it to get the same wavelength.

The issue with this is that you sacrifice your energy every time you use negative emotions as a means of contact. When you both work in a bad mood, your success rate in helping them also diminishes. When you are depressed, stressed, and sad, it is difficult to listen to others and find solutions.

However, understanding and compassion can be achieved without sacrificing energy.

Receiving Your Partner's Emotional Energy Is Not Your Responsibility.

When you take responsibility for their negative feelings and energy, it starts belonging to you, and your body, mind, and spirit will respond where you are genuinely responsible and need to be addressed.

Most often, when you are addicted and experience their stress and problems, you will feel rundown and overwhelmed. Sometimes you get sick, or it affects your work performance because you have a burden with you.

No Matter How Much You Love and Care for Your Partner, You Are Not Responsible for Their Happiness.

You should be responsible for yourself and your experiences, but you are not responsible for them if necessary. Don't think that you can help your partner with inadequate energy consumption. The best way to help your partner is to keep strong feelings and invite them to meet in a positive place.

Many clients I work within marriage counselling have found that if they let go of each other's sense of responsibility, they may seem more vulnerable and provide more services to their partner. In a positive place, you can think and take a variety of measures to help your spouse feel comfortable without having the responsibility or choice to be with another partner.

Let Go of Judging Them or Thinking That You Know Better.

When you think that you know better and try to change our partner, not only does it often backfire, it also allows their energy to infiltrate ours. If you don't want your spouse to affect your energy, then it is important to allow them to make their own choices and hold their own opinions.

Similarly, the act of judging, even if done silently to yourself, can bring in more negativity, as focusing on their negativity and what you perceive they are doing wrong puts you on the same low emotional vibe.

Give up trying to convince someone you know what is best for them or making judgments in your own mind. Your positive energy is the most powerful tool you have to live a happy and fulfilled life, so protect it!

Refuse to Give Your Power Away by Reacting.

Is your spouse always creating a drama? Are they trying to invoke a negative emotional response from you in order to get energy or attention from you? Do you allow your spouse's bad mood to dictate your own?

If you answered "yes", know that the moment you react, you give away your power.

Doing this leads to a temporary gain for them that sets the cycle in motion to repeat itself.

That won't help either of you in the long-term, especially if you want to save your marriage.

Remember, no one has power over you. They only have the power that you give to them, which is controlled by your thoughts, beliefs, and actions.

Sometimes relationships can feel like a lot of work. What once was an easy and joyful engagement with a caring compassionate other can slowly turn into an exhausting exchange of complaints and a mutual sense of deprivation and dissatisfaction?

Over time our once best friend can slowly begin to seem like an adversary, and our once biggest source of good feelings and accolades can slowly become a source of toxic feelings of falling short or not being good enough.

Fortunately, we now have a remedy to this steady decline of goodwill that befalls so many relationships.

Understanding Your Toxic Cycle:

A toxic cycle is a self-persuading merry-go-round where what one person says or does creates toxic feelings in the other person, and what the other person says or does creates toxic feelings in the first person. Couples thereby get stuck in a toxic spiral or vicious cycle that keeps them separate from the love, the closeness, and the good feelings they really want.

Emotionally focused couples' therapists have studied the steps involved in the toxic cycles that squeeze the love and connection out of relationships. They have made it easier to get out of these patterns, by giving us the tools we need to understand them, and providing us with insights into how to place our feet differently.

The individual steps in any toxic relationship cycle can be broken down in the following way:

Primary emotion: The real emotional response a person has to something their partner says or does or doesn't say or do. This emotion is often vulnerable and can make the person feel exposed or weak. It tends to be an emotion like sadness, pain/rejection, shame, or fear.

Secondary emotion: the emotional response a person has to the way their partner has made them feel (the primary emotion). This emotion is often a response to the more vulnerable emotion that makes a person feel stronger or at least makes the person feel less exposed or vulnerable. Sometimes this emotion will be one of anger, contempt, or anxiety.

Perception: The conclusion or interpretation a person makes about their partner based on their secondary emotion. If the person feels angry, they are likely to interpret their partner's behaviour as deliberate and ill-intentioned. If the person feels anxiety, they are likely to interpret their partner's behaviours as a sign of danger and bad things to come.

Behaviours: How a person acts or reacts based on their secondary emotional reaction and interpretation to their partner. If a person feels anxious in response to their partner, then they are likely to placate in order to avoid further conflict, to freeze up and go into problem-solving instead of staying engaged with their partner's feelings, or to shut down and withdraw in order to protect themselves.

When these individual steps are connected together in a chain for both partners in a relationship, they can be depicted as an infinity cycle that loops back and forth between partners in a continuous spiral:

In this case what is below the grey dotted line is also often below the threshold of a couple's awareness.

Why Couples Get Stuck:

Partners who have grown accustomed to feeling criticised or shut out by each other are mostly in touch with their more reactive secondary emotions, and not with the more vulnerable primary emotions and their underlying unmet needs. They lead conversations with angry criticism, or a tendency to anxiously withdraw, appease, or problem-solve.

However, because how they respond to their partner exacerbates the very problem that occasions the criticism or withdrawing to begin with, they get stuck in a lose-lose situation where both are unhappy.

A person who appeases and placates in order to stop the unbearable criticism from their partner, still remains hidden behind a wall of empty words and empty intentions, and this only makes the critical partner feel more alone, more disconnected, and more critical.

A person who criticises every little thing their partner does, instead of expressing an underlying need for attention or closeness, only ends up making their partner feel aversive to spending time with them and shutting down the very emotional connection they are yearning for.

Part Six:
Real Conversation
About Marriage

A marriage can only be kept and lived when both the parties are equally involved in building their lives together.

All romantic relationships go through ups and downs, and they all take work, commitment, and a willingness to adapt and change with your partner. But whether your relationship is just starting out or you've been together for years, there are steps you can take to build a healthy relationship. Even if you've experienced a lot of failed relationships in the past or struggled before to rekindle the fires of romance in your current relationship, you can learn to stay connected, find fulfilment, and enjoy lasting happiness.

A conversation and falling in love. Sometimes they start the same. Small talk is fine to a point, but there's one thing that sparks a connection more than any other – mutual vulnerability, powered by self-disclosure. This is where the real magic happens.

A number of studies have shown that to move a conversation from the surface to a little bit more, and mutual vulnerability is key. This calls for the conversation that's a little bit bolder and a little bit braver, but they are always the conversations that are exquisite to be a part of.

Nobody is suggesting that hearts and souls be put on the line in the name of intoxicating conversation, but intelligent, interesting conversation, with a little bit more of someone brave enough to go there, is impossible to walk away from. It's charming, fascinating, and energetic, and so are the people involved. At least that's how they will be seen and remembered.

There is an abundance of research that has looked at the way people develop intimacy. When two people begin a relationship, each begins to 'include the other in the self'. By opening up to another person's beliefs, feelings, ideology, resources, and personality, the unique parts of another are added to the already defined parts of the self, and the self-expands.

The process of self-expansion typically happens through time spent together, sharing activities, ideas, and interests. The more two people share in a novel and challenging activity, the greater the feeling of closeness. Conversation – the right conversation – can be as novel and challenging as anything.

Who doesn't want to feel more connection, love, collaboration, and better conflict resolution in their relationship? We're trying this new weekly check-in exercise as we've both been so busy with traveling lately! We're not perfect, but if there's one thing that has always strengthened our marriage is communication. Exercises like this are GOOD, and we here at The Good Life want you all to live a better life, so grab your partner and join us! If you're single—don't worry, we'll tell you why this is an exercise great for everyone. Plus, we're catching you up on a few things that happened this week and an emotional Stevie walking down memory lane at the mall? It's about to get good.

There are a few specific days throughout the course of your life that are major mile-markers. That is life-defining, life-changing days where everything shifts, and nothing is ever the same again. If you choose to get married, your wedding day is one of those moments. For most, their weddings are glorious celebrations of what is to come—the joining together of two lives as people say to each other and to the world that together, they will be better than they were apart.

But weddings don't last, marriage does. Your first dance may be memorable, but it's the dozens of times you dance together in the comfort of your own home that will define who you are, not the three minutes you spend together on that first night. Your meal may be delicious and the wedding cake delectable, but the savoury flavours of that night have nothing on the hundreds of meals that you will share across the dinner table, the Tuesday nights, and the Saturday morning brunches.

Everyone spends so much time and attention to the wedding, making sure that each detail is in place and accounted for. The invitations are handled with great care, and the seating arrangements are analysed with the precision of a master cartographer. But in the middle of such great focus, it is easy to miss the necessity of looking past the singular day to the years of marriage that lie beyond that fantastic wedding day.

Part of the preparation for marriage is having real conversations with your soon-to-be spouse that reveal the true elements of who you both are. You don't have to tell every first date you ever take to dinner your entire life story, but if you are about to commit your life to someone, for better or worse, in a commitment that many still see to be until death, you deserve to know the depths of each other. You deserve to have at least these five conversations, as knowing your spouse in these ways will greatly help the quality of your marriage.

Are You Headed in the Same Direction?

Another way to say this is, "What are your respective missions, and do they cross over?" Notice that I did not say that you and your spouse have to want the exact same things from life. There is a reason why opposites attract and that people often date and marry those who challenge and stretch their perceptions of the world around them.

While you don't need to be 100% aligned in all areas of your future, you do need to be headed in a relatively similar direction as your soon-to-be spouse. If you are planning to become a doctor and you think that the next ten years will include school, more school, and a mountain of debt to be paid off, while your partner thought it would be fun to move to Paris and live on love, you may have two very different and conflicting ideas of where you are headed.

Your mission in your marriage ultimately comes down to identifying what is important to you and thinking through how you plan to pursue that matter. If you and your partner can identify ways that you can overlap your pursuits, if you foresee opportunities to lean towards each other as you both chase down what makes your hearts come alive if you see your paths converging more than they diverge, then go for it.

What Does Family Mean to You?

This conversation comes in two main forms—extended family and kids. Everyone longs to be a part of a family, even if your experiences of family dynamics are tense and full of pain and regret. Understanding where your partner is coming from with their family, or getting to know their extended family, if possible, will be of immense value as you journey together into marriage.

People express that desire for a family in very different ways. Some people are home and present for every opportunity of celebration. You would be shocked to hear what occasions some families celebrate. And yet other people are mostly content to hardly talk to their families, let alone see them.

In that same conversation, think about broaching the topic of kids. When, how many, rough ideas on parenting. This conversation gets more important the older you get while dating, but it is still not essential to be extremely detailed while dating. However, the broad strokes of this talk help couples make sure they are at least aligned on the basics. These conversations help bring up some hard but necessary topics such as when each person wants to start trying to have kids or what each person's views are towards infertility and or adoption should there be trouble conceiving.

Talking about these family topics before you get married allows for both you and your future spouse to have a framework to stand on when the "family" conversations start becoming more and more pressing.

A marriage without conflict is not a marriage. It is an unexplored form of appeasement. This in no means implies that you have to fight constantly, or that conflict is always a good thing. But to disagree and to feel conflict is human. It doesn't mean that you are a bad person, it means that you care and you are willing to engage to the point of learning that you can be wrong about your opinions.

Before you get married, it's important to understand how your partner views and handles conflict. Do they like to sweep things under the rug, or are they someone who comes out, fists swinging, looking for a fight? Are you quiet, moody, and passive-aggressive when you are upset, or do you become loud and angry? Arguments are inevitable—that much we know for certain. But it's how a couple handles that conflict that determines whether or not they will continue to be healthy moving forward.

Conflict is cyclical. You do something that frustrates your partner, and they frustrate you back. You push their button, and they push yours. On and on. You need to talk ahead of time about how you may break the cycle at the moment. Maybe that means space. Maybe that means physical contact like a hug or a gentle hand on the shoulder.

Part of the conflict conversation is coming to a realisation of the role you play in any argument. Regardless of if you started the conflict or just got involved in it, you can still learn to be a positive influence in resolving that conflict with grace and kindness.

If you genuinely trust your partner, this is a question you only need to ask once. Before you commit your life to someone, before you take those vows and stand before God and your family and pledge to love each other unconditionally, give each other the opportunity to be totally vulnerable and honest. I've heard this described as the "deal breaker and bucket-list conversation". It is wise to go into this conversation with the right attitude, one of humility and non-judgment.

For most couples, it is not necessary to know every sordid detail of the past. Each of us has mistaken and scars that we are not proud of. But there needs to be a moment before you are married where you and your partner can share the deepest levels of who you are and voice, if you haven't already, anything that you think your spouse would be sad or frustrated to learn after your wedding.

If you are wondering what those an example may be of something a person could share with their partner, it's likely that part of your story that comes to mind when you think about the thing you most desperately do not want to share or let anyone find out about, ever. For most people in the western world, marriage is a choice, and there are few things more powerful than choosing to love someone regardless of their past.

Each conversation is important to have before you get married. But even once you are married, these conversations do not go away. You may not need to ask your spouse, "Is there anything else I need to know?" but you do need to continue to practice the rhythms of repentance and forgiveness, admitting your mistakes and choosing to love one another in spite of what you both have done.

You do need to continue to talk about money, about mission, family, and conflict. Most weddings go off without a hitch, but many marriages steer off course because these conversations and so many more are never truly present. Talk before and keep talking. You'll only be stronger because of it.

Don't tear down another person with your words. Instead, keep the peace, and be considerate. Be truly humble toward everyone. Consideration means that you think about your spouse's opinion, and you value their thoughts. You are truly listening to understand rather than waiting for your turn to make your point. Years ago, when we were having a hard time waiting to adopt our second child, I wanted to just stop the process and presented my husband my arguments so that he would see things the way I did. Looking back now, I am so thankful that I listened to my husband and considered everything he was thinking and feeling – this led to us patiently waiting until we were able to adopt our daughter at eight weeks old.

Do you have conversations to understand your spouse in order to be unified, or do you approach your spouse trying to convince and persuade?

It takes courage to speak the truth and to listen to the truth. Last year we felt stuck in our marriage; we knew we weren't growing or changing. I was fearful in our conversations and not honest about the needs I had, the struggles I was facing, or the hurts I was feeling in our marriage. I was also too afraid to hear how my husband was really feeling towards me – he felt I was always rushing ahead, trying to prove myself rather than wanting to be close to him. We had many honest conversations that were painful for both of us, but they led to us being aware of each other's needs and the negative impact we were having on one another. These talks led to changes in our marriage by making each other a priority over ourselves and our own agendas.

Are you willing to face truths about yourself, your spouse, and your marriage so that you can change and grow closer? Having the courage, to be honest about deeper and more vulnerable parts of ourselves will prevent our marriages from getting distant.

Throughout our marriage, we have had many long conversations that made us feel more distant than close and connected. Often compassion was missing in these times, and resentment made us both feel like the other person was not going to understand. It has helped our marriage for each of us to ask God to help us be compassionate towards the other person and to understand their struggles and challenges. Having compassion on your spouse helps you not take everything personally and realise that we need each other to overcome our weaknesses. The resolution takes two people with compassion and willingness to let go of wrongs.

Do you start your conversations with a compassionate view of your spouse? Or do you start conversations already assuming your spouse won't understand you?

Whether we are newly married or have had many years together, consideration, courage, and compassion can help us have conversations that strengthen our marriages.

What your now-spouse found sexy about you from the start was your individuality, points out house. And it was those interesting, individual interests, quirks, and stories you likely gabbed on about. Complement each other and make sure they're authentic niceties that go deeper than how great he or she looks in his or her new outfit. Saying "how smart they are, or mentioning what amazing curiosity they have or their admirable dedication, is disarming". "We may have put protective walls up without even realising it. If we feel safe, appreciated, and supported, we can allow those walls to come down again, and we can open up emotionally, therefore having more conversations about deeper, more meaningful things."

Your after-work chats might not be the same. If you think there's a deeper reason—such as a relationship disconnect—that you're not talking as much to one another, it's okay to gently address the lack of flow in your conversations. You can, for example, "tell your partner, 'I know some things have been building with me that I'd like to talk to you about. And I would imagine that the same holds true for you, so let's figure out a way we can make it safe enough to talk about these issues,'".

Then set up a new conversation routine in which you each don't interrupt, repeat back what your partner says, and work to keep the conversation on track.

Like with anything in life, relationships have stages. And although a guidebook that pinpoints the exact right moment for every milestone would be mega helpful, the truth is, every duo moves at a pace that's right for them. That's why it can be a very tricky situation when you're ready to cement your lifelong commitment with engagement—and your partner isn't quite there yet. The healthiest and happiest of relationships thrive off of communication and the willingness to discuss every nook and cranny of your mind and heart.

You and your person have been together for so many years, you both lose count. Or you've only shared one lap around the sun together—but it feels like you've known one another forever. Whatever the case, when you move from being boyfriend-girlfriend (or BF-BF and GF-GF) to engage, you up the ante on intimacy. And that's scary. As a licensed professional counsellor specialising in couples therapy, the concept itself comes with built-in vulnerability and the possibility of rejection. "You're laying it all out there, and your partner may not feel the same. What if you don't see eye to eye? What if your partner wants something different? What if they have a different vision of what the future looks like?"

"You might discover you are not as ready as you thought. In having a conversation about getting engaged, there is the possibility of disappointment because you both may discover you are not on the same page after all."

Some parties within the relationship avoid discussing the topic at all, since they don't want to be perceived as a "nag", or come across as annoying or pushy. Most ladies traditionally want to be proposed to as well, so they worry about announcing they want to get engaged because it could ruin the element of a romantic surprise.

No matter how anxious it may make you—or that person you wake up to every morning—Bradshaw deems the convo as healthy. And having conversations about the future is something to practice time and time again—think of it as a check-in. "It's not a one-and-done thing; it's many conversations over time. You'll be confident in your future together once you've discussed engagement and marriage thoroughly and clearly define where you both stand on the subject and see how you view your future together."

Be Mindful of the Timing

A certain number of years or months of dating, but rather, your surroundings and what's happening in your personal lives. A dinner party isn't the smartest setting for a super-serious, are-we-going-to-get-hitched discussion. After all, marriage at its core is about joining two lives together—not just a sparkly diamond or big party. "Maybe you're ready to plant roots and want to move out of your apartment and into a house that's in a good neighbourhood with a great school. Maybe you want to ditch the two-door sports car and get something more practical for a life that is evolving. Maybe you want to take that trip that you know will not be practical if you have kids, so perhaps discussing that dream trip is how you start that conversation." "The bottom line is that timing will help you, as well as the entry point you choose to bring up the conversation."

Acknowledge it's weird because it may feel that way at first. Getting the "I know this is difficult to talk about but..." out of the way, in the beginning, can make it easier to speak freely. "Express that it seems like the time has come, at least for you, to express how you feel about your significant other and where you feel you are in the relationship. By letting your partner know this is hard for you to talk about too, it may encourage them to also have the courage, to be honest back with you."

Express your love. The desire to get engaged really boils down to the fact that you can't imagine your life with anyone else. Especially if you fret over coming across as clingy or knaggy, being straightforward about how deeply you love your partner can send the right message and illustrate how well you work as a team. "Share your dreams with your partner. Those dreams can be visions of vacations, where you'll live, how you'll celebrate special occasions and holidays, how you envision spending your free time together, things you want to do together that you have yet to do, and things you are looking forward to doing." "By talking about your dreams, you are indirectly stating that you see both of you together for the long haul, and that can segue into a conversation about marriage."

Since you're fishing around to better understand where your partner is on your relationship journey, open-ended questions can help you arrive at answers. You should be careful of being hypersensitive toward their answers, since sometimes, it doesn't have anything to do with you, but a notion your partner has come up with all by themselves. "Seek to understand their reasons for it versus taking it personally. It's just a different opinion at the moment of discussion and is not necessarily a reflection of the status of the future of your relationship, nor is it necessarily a direct reflection of you as a partner. You want to be able to directly communicate your reasons for wanting to get married, why taking your relationship to the next level is important, and why it feels right to you. If you are able to clearly express your reasons for this, your partner is more likely to be open to hearing your thoughts on the subject."

Like with anything in life, relationships have stages. And although a guidebook that pinpoints the exact right moment for every milestone would be mega helpful, the truth is, every duo moves at a pace that's right for them. That's why it can be a very tricky situation when you're ready to cement your lifelong commitment with engagement—and your partner isn't quite there yet. The healthiest and happiest of relationships thrive off of communication and the willingness to discuss every nook and cranny of your mind and heart.

But even if you and your number one are incredibly open with one another, bringing up the, "Hey, should we put a ring on it?" discussion can cause jitters in anyone. Psychologists weighed in on how to navigate this chat, so couples don't have to stress.

Talk about your relationship dreams or, in other words: Express your love. The desire to get engaged really boils down to the fact that you can't imagine your life with anyone else. Especially if you fret over coming across as clingy or knaggy, being straightforward about how deeply you love your partner can send the right message and illustrate how well you work as a team. "Share your dreams with your partner. Those dreams can be visions of vacations, where you'll live, how you'll celebrate special occasions and holidays, how you envision spending your free time together, things you want to do together that you have yet to do, and things you are looking forward to doing." "By talking about your dreams, you are indirectly stating that you see both of you together for the long haul, and that can segue into a conversation about marriage."

Building a Healthy Relationship

Every relationship is unique, and people come together for many different reasons. Part of what defines a healthy relationship is sharing a common goal for exactly what you want the relationship to be and where you want it to go. And that's something you'll only know by talking deeply and honestly with your partner. However, there are also some characteristics that most healthy relationships have in common. Knowing these basic principles can help keep your relationship meaningful, fulfilling, and exciting whatever goals you're working towards or challenges you're facing together.

You maintain a meaningful emotional connection with each other. You each make the other feel loved and emotionally fulfilled. There's a difference between being loved and feeling loved. When you feel loved, it makes you feel accepted and valued by your partner, like someone truly gets you. Some relationships get stuck in peaceful coexistence, but without the partners truly relating to each other emotionally. While the union may seem stable on the surface, a lack of ongoing involvement and emotional connection serves only to add distance between two people.

You're not afraid of (respectful) disagreement. Some couples talk things out quietly, while others may raise their voices and passionately disagree. The key in a strong relationship, though, is not to be fearful of conflict. You need to feel safe to express things that bother you without fear of retaliation and be able to resolve conflict without humiliation, degradation, or insisting on being right.

You keep outside relationships and interests alive. Despite the claims of romantic fiction or movies, no one person can meet all of your needs. In fact, expecting too much from your partner can put unhealthy pressure on a relationship. To stimulate and enrich your romantic relationship, it's important to sustain your own identity outside of the relationship, preserve connections with family and friends, and maintain your hobbies and interests.

You communicate openly and honestly. Good communication is a key part of any relationship. When both people know what they want from the relationship and feel comfortable expressing their needs, fears, and desires, it can increase trust and strengthen the bond between you.

Falling in Love Vs Staying in Love

For most people, falling in love usually seems to just happen. It's staying in love—or preserving that "falling in love" experience—that requires commitment and work. Given its rewards, though, it's well worth the effort. A healthy, secure romantic relationship can serve as an ongoing source of support and happiness in your life, through good times and bad, strengthening all aspects of your wellbeing. By taking steps now to preserve or rekindle your falling in love experience, you can build a meaningful relationship that lasts—even for a lifetime.

Many couples focus on their relationship only when there are specific, unavoidable problems to overcome. Once the problems have been resolved, they often switch their attention back to their careers, kids, or other interests. However, romantic relationships require ongoing attention and commitment for love to flourish. As long as the health of a romantic relationship remains important to you, it is going to require your attention and effort. And identifying and fixing a small problem in your relationship now can often help prevent it from growing into a much larger one down the road. The following tips can help you to preserve that falling in love experience and keep your romantic relationship healthy.

You fall in love looking at and listening to each other. If you continue to look and listen in the same attentive ways, you can sustain the falling in love experience over the long term. You probably have fond memories of when you were first dating your loved one. Everything seemed new and exciting, and you likely spent hours just chatting together or coming up with new, exciting things to try. However, as time goes by, the demands of work, family, other obligations, and the need we all have for time to ourselves can make it harder to find time together.

Many couples find that the face-to-face contact of their early dating days is gradually replaced by hurried texts, emails, and instant messages. While digital communication is great for some purposes, it doesn't positively impact your brain and nervous system in the same way as face-to-face communication. Sending a text or a voice message to your partner saying "I love you" is great, but if you rarely look at them or have the time to sit down together, they'll still feel you don't understand or appreciate them. And you'll become more distanced or disconnected as a couple. The emotional cues you both need to feel loved can only be conveyed in person, so no matter how busy life gets, it's important to carve out time to spend together.

Commit to spending some quality time together on a regular basis. No matter how busy you are, take a few minutes each day to put aside your electronic devices, stop thinking about other things, and really focus on and connect with your partner.

Find something that you enjoy doing together, whether it is a shared hobby, dance class, daily walk, or sitting over a cup of coffee in the morning.

Try something new together. Doing new things together can be a fun way to connect and keep things interesting. It can be as simple as trying a new restaurant or going on a day trip to a place you've never been to before.

Focus on having fun together. Couples are often more fun and playful in the early stages of a relationship. However, this playful attitude can sometimes be forgotten as life challenges start getting in the way or old resentments start building up.

Keeping a sense of humour can actually help you get through tough times, reduce stress, and work through issues more easily. Think about playful ways to surprise your partner, like bringing flowers home or unexpectedly booking a table at their favourite restaurant. Playing with pets or small children can also help you reconnect with your playful side.

Good communication is a fundamental part of a healthy relationship. When you experience a positive emotional connection with your partner, you feel safe and happy. When people stop communicating well, they stop relating well, and times of change or stress can really bring out the disconnect. It may sound simplistic, but as long as you are communicating, you can usually work through whatever problems you're facing.

Tell your partner what you need, don't make them guess. It's not always easy to talk about what you need. For one, many of us don't spend enough time thinking about what's really important to us in a relationship. And even if you do know what you need, talking about it can make you feel vulnerable, embarrassed, or even ashamed. But look at it from your partner's point of view. Providing comfort and understanding to someone you love is a pleasure, not a burden.

If you've known each other for a while, you may assume that your partner has a pretty good idea of what you are thinking and what you need. However, your partner is not a mind-reader. While your partner may have some idea, it is much healthier to express your needs directly to avoid any confusion. Your partner may sense something, but it might not be what you need. What's more, people change, and what you needed and wanted five years ago, for example, may be very different now. So instead of letting resentment, misunderstanding, or anger grow when your partner continually gets it wrong, get in the habit of telling them exactly what you need.

Take note of your partner's nonverbal cues. So much of our communication is transmitted by what we don't say. Nonverbal cues, which include eye contact, tone of voice, posture, and gestures such as leaning forward, crossing your arms, or touching someone's hand, communicate much more than words. When you can pick up on your partner's nonverbal cues or "body language", you'll be able to tell how they really feel and be able to respond accordingly. For a relationship to work well, each person has to understand their own and their partner's nonverbal cues. Your partner's responses may be different from yours. For example, one person might find a hug after a stressful day, a loving mode of communication—while another might just want to take a walk together or sit and chat.

It's also important to make sure that what you say matches your body language. If you say, "I'm fine," but you clench your teeth and look away, then your body is clearly signalling you are anything but "fine".

When you experience positive emotional cues from your partner, you feel loved and happy, and when you send positive emotional cues, your partner feels the same. When you stop taking an interest in your own or your partner's emotions, you'll damage the connection between you and your ability to communicate will suffer, especially during stressful times.

Be a good listener, while a great deal of emphasis in our society is put on talking, if you can learn to listen in a way that makes another person feel valued and understood, you can build a deeper, stronger connection between you. There's a big difference between listening in this way and simply hearing. When you really listen—when you're engaged with what's being said—you'll hear the subtle intonations in your partner's voice that tells you how they're really feeling and the emotions they're trying to communicate. Being a good listener doesn't mean you have to agree with your partner or change your mind. But it will help you find common points of view that can help you to resolve conflict.

Keep physical intimacy alive, and touch is a fundamental part of human existence. Studies on infants have shown the importance of regular, affectionate contact for brain development. And the benefits don't end in childhood. Affectionate contact boosts the body's levels of oxytocin, a hormone that influences bonding and attachment.

While sex is often a cornerstone of a committed relationship, it shouldn't be the only method of physical intimacy. Frequent, affectionate touch—holding hands, hugging, kissing—is equally important.

Of course, it's important to be sensitive to what your partner likes. Unwanted touching or inappropriate overtures can make the other person tense up and retreat—exactly what you don't want. As with so many other aspects of a healthy relationship, this can come down to how well you communicate your needs and intentions with your partner.

Even if you have pressing workloads or young children to worry about, you can help to keep physical intimacy alive by carving out some regular couple time, whether that's in the form of a date night or simply an hour at the end of the day when you can sit and talk or hold hands.

Learn to give and take in your relationship. If you expect to get what you want 100% of the time in a relationship, you are setting yourself up for disappointment. Healthy relationships are built on compromise. However, it takes work on each person's part to make sure that there is a reasonable exchange.

Recognise what's important to your partner. Knowing what is truly important to your partner can go a long way towards building goodwill and an atmosphere of compromise. On the flip side, it's also important for your partner to recognise your wants and for you to state them clearly. Constantly giving in to others at the expense of your own needs will only build resentment and anger.

Don't make "winning" your goal. If you approach your partner with the attitude that things have to be your way or else, it will be difficult to reach a compromise. Sometimes this attitude comes from not having your needs met while younger, or it could be years of accumulated resentment in the relationship reaching a boiling point. It's alright to have strong convictions about something, but your partner deserves to be prepared for ups and downs.

It's important to recognise that there are ups and downs in every relationship. You won't always be on the same page. Sometimes one partner may be struggling with an issue that stresses them, such as the death of a close family member. Other events, like job loss or severe health problems, can affect both partners and make it difficult to relate to each other. You might have different ideas about managing finances or raising children. Different people cope with stress differently, and misunderstandings can rapidly turn to frustration and anger.

Don't take out your problems with your partner. Life stresses can make us short-tempered. If you are coping with a lot of stress, it might seem easier to vent with your partner, and even feel safer to snap at them. Fighting like this might initially feel like a release, but it slowly poisons your relationship. Find other healthier ways to manage your stress, anger, and frustration.

Trying to force a solution can cause even more problems. Every person works through problems and issues in their own way. Remember that you're a team. Continuing to move forward together can get you through the rough spots.

Look back to the early stages of your relationship. Share the moments that brought the two of you together, examine the point at which you began to drift apart, and resolve how you can work together to rekindle that falling in love experience.

Be open to change. Change is inevitable in life, and it will happen whether you go with it or fight it. Flexibility is essential to adapt to the change that is always taking place in any relationship, and it allows you to grow together through both the good times and the bad.

If you need outside help for your relationship, reach out together. Sometimes problems in a relationship can seem too complex or overwhelming for you to handle as a couple. Couples therapy or talking together with a trusted friend or religious figure can help. To be heard as well. Be respectful of the other person and their viewpoint.

Part Seven:
What Feeds Hatred
in Relationships?

While every relationship goes through ups and downs, there are a number of relationships that transition into toxicity. Some relationships become unpleasing and start to drain people in it to a point that their negative moments outweigh their positive relationship. A relationship between two people who fail to support each other or solve conflicts between each other soon leads to separation.

A toxic relationship is one that makes you feel unsupported, misunderstood, demeaned, or attacked. On a basic level, any relationship that makes you feel worse rather than better can become toxic over time. Toxic relationships can exist in just about any context, from the playground to the boardroom to the bedroom. You may even deal with toxic relationships among your family members.

When determining if a relationship is creating toxicity, it is important to look at which behaviours are being displayed most frequently in the relationship. In other words, if one or both of you are consistently selfish, negative, and disrespectful, you could be creating toxicity in the relationship. But if you're mostly encouraging, compassionate, and respectful, then there might just be certain issues that create toxicity that need to be addressed.

It's important to recognise the signs of toxicity—whether it's in you or in the other person. It's important to note that toxic relationships are not limited to romantic relationships. They exist in families, in the workplace, and among friend groups—and they can be extremely stressful, especially if the toxicity isn't effectively managed.

Not all toxic relationships are caused by both parties. Some people are simply toxic to be around—they sap your energy with negative behaviours like constant complaining, critical remarks, and overall negativity. Or, they may argue with others constantly, explain why they know better, or point out the flaws of others—all of which may weigh on you over time.

Sometimes people act this way toward everyone and are unaware of their effect on others. They also may not know healthier ways to communicate. It's likely that they don't know how to read social cues well enough to know when they're frustrating people or making them feel like they are being criticised or ignored.

But other times, people are deliberately rude and hurtful. In these situations, you may feel singled out and targeted through their mean words and actions. And, no matter what you do, you feel like you're never measuring up or good enough.

If these scenarios are true of your situation, you may want to re-evaluate your relationship with this person. They may be causing real damage to your self-esteem and your overall mental health as well as your physical health.

How to Transform Hate into Love in Your Relationships

Love, such a warm fuzzy feeling encompassing you. You feel secure, happy and euphoric. And then it happens. You have something on your mind that's bothering you and you want to talk to your partner about it. You bring up the topic quite innocently, unaware that you are about to step on a landmine and set off an intense emotional chain reaction.

Instead of answering your question as you expected, your partner dismisses the very notion of your query and relates to it negatively. You are offended and try more strongly to explain to him that it is important to you. The more you try to explain, the more he stands his ground, and the more his point of view makes you angry. Words turn into blame, and emotion replaces your sense of reason. You default into criticism, clamming him up…

And there you have it: Hate. In a matter of minutes, without much warning, love becomes hate. The person most close to you becomes the most distant.

Your shared space is now a war zone. You can't stand each other's presence. Your egos want to erase the source of angst now threatening your sense of self. The inner mechanism constantly calculating your gains and losses just can't bear to lose. How on earth, did you go from being two love doves to enemies, in a flash?

Is it hormones? Is it just that time of the month? Or is it communication skills, his lack of empathy, your insensitivity? Over the years I realised that it's none of the above. There is something else at work, of much greater significance.

The Laws of the Network

For a long time, I studied the patterns in my relationships. I noticed how love and hate, connection and separation would come and go in unexpected ways. Like a volcano erupting or a hail storm, an argument would pop out of seemingly nowhere and leave destruction in its wake.

I noticed that I was not in control of this ebb and flow, that just like the powers of nature, like the weather, my relationships were also influenced by these hidden forces.

After having fights with my partner, I often discovered it was not just me. Friends around me were also experiencing similar things. Something was going on here that was beyond my own private emotional life. For years, Social Psychology has been saying that though we think we are living separate, independent lives, we are in fact influenced by the social network we are part of in ways we cannot fathom. We influence each other through the network with our behaviour's, thoughts, emotions, our love, and hate. So, whenever we feel upset, negative, or imbalanced, it is really no coincidence.

Beyond the circumstances of whatever we are fighting about, and as convincing as the supposed reason for being angry is, there is a network in which we all live that is influencing us in every moment. My anger and frustration are the result of negative emotion going around the network. It gets even more interesting because according to the wisdom of Kabbalah, which is a science of connected systems, the network also has a life of its own! It is ruled by the law of love, and like a great superorganism, it is undergoing a process of development, and it is taking us with it, towards greater interconnection and eventual harmony.

The pressures we feel are this network's way of pressing us towards higher levels of connection. It creates these dramas in our lives as a way to make us grow. This is where we need to be very aware of how the system is operating on us. We mustn't for a moment think that what is happening to us is a matter of coincidence. We must remember that any event, good or bad, and especially hate or turmoil is really coming to us from the network…as an invitation!

It's an invitation for growth, and for greater connection.

Growing with the Flow

When you remember that what you are experiencing is not yours at all, but coming from a higher system of which we are part, you attain a special awareness that allows you to divert your anger and work above it.

Instead of attacking your partner for his behaviours, you do not relate to what is happening directly. Instead, you go above it.

You resist your automatic response, to convince, to protest, to blame or argue.

And when both of you make this effort to resist your automatic response, remembering where everything is coming from and for what purpose—something amazing happens!

Above the layer of resistance that you created, a new quality of love and partnership appears.

Just as in any battery, plus and minus connect with a resistor between them.

This is nature's mechanism for creating energy, and power. Thus, any relationship can turn into a powerhouse, taking the negative inputs, converting them and infusing the system with positive inputs in return. In this way, all the other people who are connected to you will receive this power which will make it easier for them to remember this game and work above their anger too.

The Step-by-Step Antidote to Hate and Negativity

Here is the summary and step-by-step action plan.
When negativity appears in your relationship:

1. Realise what's going on. Whenever a negative situation evolves within your relationship, remember, it's not YOU, and it's not THEM. It's an OPPORTUNITY you just received from the network, to discover more love, and GROW as a couple.

2. Don't believe your subjective perception. Once you have acknowledged that what is happening is no one's fault, try to rise above the blame that may be going on within you towards your partner. Remember that however things may look right now, however bad (rude, insensitive, mean or repulsive, etc, etc.) your partner may seem to you, this is temporary! It is just a passing state, which will completely change when it is over. Don't buy into it!

3. Resist the temptation of automatic responses. As hard as it is to avoid it, trying to solve the situation by explaining, convincing or demanding to get your point across is mostly futile. Remember the whole point of the situation is to resist the hate and discover more love. The mission is to rise above the situation. Not to get riddled in the details. Later, once the

emotion has subsided, you can talk to your partner about what is important to you in the relationship. Right now, though, resist the urge to criticise.

4. Feel the freedom. Now that you are resisting your automatic impulses you should begin to sense relief from the situation's hold on you. You have gained higher awareness.

5. Hug it out. Ask your partner for a hug, to show that you want to go above the situation. As you hug, sense that a new point of connection is created between you. The problem at hand has become your common enemy, helping you two unite and be more deeply connected to each other thanks to it.

6. Congratulate yourself and your partner! You have succeeded at converting hate into love, and the whole human network is indebted to you!

7. Accepting failure. If you have failed somewhere along these steps, don't worry about it. This process takes time to master, and often it takes many failed attempts in which you try to solve the situation "the regular way", (which means trying to change your partner, or fight the situation away) which don't work 99.9% of the time, to finally decide to work above it. When you have finally decided that nothing is going to work except for loving your partner as they are, and rising above whatever negative impulses arise in you, you WILL succeed!

A Time for Change

In our world today we hear about so much hate. Hate crimes, violence, divorce. all of these are symptoms of a network of connection that is saturated with negative thoughts, emotions, and actions.

We must learn how to work with the negative forces within us, to make them work for us.

This work takes practice. We need to change our wiring and learn to love above our hate. But once we master this science, we can use negative emotions as an engine for positive transformation, creating balance and ripples of happiness all around us!

Part Eight:
Important Qualities for a
Happy Marriage

In the current world, finding a couple breaking their rules for each other in the name of love becomes breaking news across the globe. What we don't realise is that we are ready to fantasise something but would never implement it. We would look at someone compromising or going out of their way for their soulmate and wish someone would do the same for us. That's where we're wrong. Instead of wondering if someone would be willing to do the same thing for us, why don't we ask ourselves if we're willing to do that for someone else?

Since when does a crisis mean the end of a marriage? We've become so quick to give up on something we once were ready to fight for. You can't weather a storm if you're not willing to stand and face it. Yes, it may be scary, and you might suffer some blows as well, but that is the price everyone pays for love, and it is okay. In fact, it's worth it. But let's face it, the things in our life that mean the most are the things we fought for and suffered for. Your marriage comes to matter because you suffered for it. When you hold onto something through the suffering, you grow a root. You develop a depth of appreciation that you can't get without suffering. It's on the other side of the pain and suffering that the most beautiful people and marriages are made.

Here are **7 important qualities** for a happy marriage:

Loyalty

When you build a wall, it is supposed to stay intact because you trust the foundation it's built on. The very ground you walk on, is a platform you trust. Imagine living and building a life with someone who has zero loyalty towards you? That is one of the scariest drawbacks of a marriage. However, the best way to have a happy marriage is to focus on what you have and what you lack. The truth is, you cannot fix someone. You can only fix yourself.

It can be said that loyalty is very important to the success, and stability of any lasting relationship. Be it business or marriage, being loyal is defined as "being faithful to one's oath, engagements or obligations".

Man and woman, who remain faithful to marital vows, stay together and strive for each other's well-being. It is important to take a big step towards marital loyalty.

As a trustworthy contractor would never start a construction without first consulting the blueprint, a person in a marriage can only be successful in making it a happy one if they pay close attention to its blue print as well.

The secret to having a lasting relationship for many couples is loyalty, a much praised and less widely practiced quality.

You deserve someone who is truly yours. Someone whom you'd offer the world and they'd say they have you. Similarly, they do too.

Responsibility

When you vow to spend your lives together. You often forget that marrying someone isn't a proof of your love or commitment, it is simply a step towards it. Your actions and attitude towards them daily is what proves whether your vows and promises were real or just empty.

A married life brings along a lot of responsibilities. In fact, marriage itself is a responsibility. You cannot just stop being responsible about it one day. A marriage isn't just spending lives together. It's about equal opportunities and responsibilities. You cannot just overburden someone else and relax on the couch. It demands a sense of responsibility and equality. Therefore, divide your chores, help each other and make sure none of you are unjust to the other.

If there's one thing common in every quality mentioned in this book, it's the attribute of being just to someone you love. If a marriage doesn't stand on the grounds of justice, it is bound to fall and break into pieces.

It is important for you to treat someone the way you expect to be treated.

Respect

Respect in marriage is one of the most important denominators of marital health and resilience. The notion of respect cuts across both scientific and spiritual conceptions of marital intimacy. Marital satisfaction and a sense of "we-ness" are contingent upon the respect that spouses show toward one another.

Respect is an attribute that is required in almost every relationship, especially marriage. Respect isn't just in the tone or words you speak, it reflects through your actions and perceptions as well.

If you carry out an act that reflects injustice, inequality and or any kind of arrogance, it is a sign that you do not respect your soulmate. Why else would you find it okay to carry out such an act?

Respect is essential. There's no compromise over it. You cannot look down upon someone who has equal importance in your house, life and marriage. Respect also means respecting someone's values. When you live together, especially in a marriage. There will come a time you'll have to put down some thoughts, habits and etc. because they do not align with your partners' values. The thing is, you wouldn't want your partner to do something you're extremely against or that hurts your feelings. Then why should you?

Respect each other, it makes more room for love.

Faith

Faith is just another word of trust here. The thing is, there's really no point of staying together if you're not able to trust someone. How would you sleep at night peacefully when your significant other said he's away for business purposes? How would you be able to distinguish between right and wrong when your judgement could be clouded? Trust is essential.

When you vow to each other, it's because you're willing to keep that promise. Along with trust comes space, which is also required in every relationship. You cannot spy on your partner, that's unethical and disrespecting. Trust the promise you both made. Have faith in the promise you and your partner made. The truth is, evil lurks everywhere. And there will be times when the situation might scream a story against your partner, but have faith. Faith is going to save your marriage when nothing else can.

Faith is a foundation that does not allow the steps of evil. It grows intimacy, and loyalty among each other. Having faith is what helps staying hopeful even in the darkest days.

Where there is love, there always has to be a leap of faith.

Confidence

Once there's faith and trust in a couple, there's always going to be confidence. You'll stand your ground no matter what the circumstances. Even if a storm comes your way, you'll be ready together. Be confident about the person you're with. Make them your strength, be their strength. There's no way you can survive the rough times if you're not willing to be each other's bullet-proof jacket. Stand up for each other, that's the way it goes.

Apart from being confident about your partner, it is important for you to be confident about yourself. Lack of confidence increases insecurities and doubts that can come between your relationships. A lack of self-confidence leads to less self-care and self-love.

This can lead to petty fights and a communication gap as well. How would you be able to communicate and express your feelings when you aren't self-confident? How would you be able to lead a married social life if you're not confident about yourself?

Lack of self-confidence can build up toxic traits due to insecurities. Love yourself, no matter what.

You're not really fit to love someone else when you're not able to love yourself.

Hope

Hope is a quality that is firstly required in an individual, then in a couple. Without hope, each fight might lead to the end of marriage. This is because hope gives one the ability to not give up. It gives us the strength to keep going no matter what how rough the tides are. Having hope as an individual is a different thing and having hope in a couple is an entirely different thing.

How do you keep moving forward when your mind convinces you there's nothing in the end? How do you stop yourself from giving up?

Hope. When you find no rope to hold on to, just hope.

The power of hope is inevitable. It keeps you walking in the darkness in search of light. And regardless of there being light or darkness in the end, what it does best is that it helps you cross the darkness. You do move on, you do go past it.

Hope, because sometimes, that is the only thing that keeps you going.

Teamwork

Teamwork isn't just a quality, it's an asset; without which a marriage is, indeed, at loss. The moment you marry someone, you have vowed to be their support system. What is the purpose of marriage if there isn't any teamwork? What's the point of living with someone if you still have an individual's approach?

The thing is, when you enter a marriage, you aren't just about to share your responsibilities, but in fact, you're about to share your opportunities as well. You don't have to just be there for each other in times of need. It's the happiness that you share which reflects real love.

It is said, you always remember the one who loves you in times of despair. And you always remember the one you love when you're happy.

Support each other. Bend for one another. If one falls down, get down and pick them up. Grow together, rise together and learn together.

In a marriage, you're a team, there's no sides. If one falls, both get hurt.

Ending Note

If you've been missing out on any of the above-mentioned attributes and points, I'd suggest you practice them. Marriage is an essential part of life. It can either make you, or break you. If you have children, then there might be more than two lives at stake. Besides, where there's love, a little bit of bending of the rules shouldn't even be considered as a compromise or sacrifice. That's just love, mate. Good Luck!